To Duncan
From Erwin
Xmas 1988
£1.50
£ ART
/PA

A View From
The Stands

(*Or:* The Amateur Concert
Wrecker's Handbook)

by
Peter Akehurst

Nova Music Limited
Goldsmid Mews
15a Farm Road
Hove
East Sussex BN3 1FB

for Norman
with gratitude for his help and encouragement

Cover Design by Martin Goodman
Illustrator Tim Fawcett
Typesetting by ac Typesetting Services, Hove, East Sussex
Printed by Nova Music Limited, Hove, East Sussex

Contents

Page

Tuning In..5

Opening The Score...7

Pricing Yourself Into The Market..9

Sowing The Seeds of Chaos..14

Drifting With The Wind...18

The Finishing Touches 21

A Foretaste of Disaster..27

Your Worst Fears Realised..33

Playing Away From Home...39

Moving Into The Small Time...44

Picking Up The Pieces..51

Some Sharp Practice..59

Prelude
Tuning In

Most of my experience as an amateur musician has been gained while squinting along the fingerboard of a viola. As a result, what follows in these pages may show a certain bias towards that instrument in particular, and towards strings in general. I am sorry if any pianists or wind players feel that their art has been neglected. No offence towards them is intended, and I have done my best to insult them wherever possible.

I would like to take this opportunity to thank in advance any of my friends who read this book, and are still prepared to play chamber music with me. (If the situation were reversed I certainly would not play with them.)

Any resemblance between characters described here and real people is of course purely accidental. However, as there are so many coincidences in life, I have changed a few names now and then to protect the guilty, and discourage libel suits.

Overture

Opening The Score

If you receive a violent blow on the knee-cap from an instrument case in a crowded train, you can be sure the owner will fall into one of two categories – Musicians or Amateurs. Both perform in evening dress, but there the similarity ends.

Musicians belong to orchestras with a full complement of players, execute all the notes written by composers, and get paid for their efforts. They are a dull bunch – but don't worry, I shall not mention them again.

Amateurs belong to orchestras that lack crucial players, take little notice of anything that composers have written, but enjoy life to the full. They can be further divided into two groups – Duffers and Bluffers. Neither can play well, but the latter have learned to conceal their shortcomings.

Emily is a typical Duffer. She is a fiddle player with a great deal of charm, and absolutely no talent for music.

A few years ago she was playing in a concert, and had a stand to herself at the back of the seconds. The concert included a piano concerto. When the soloist started his cadenza, a shrill whine like an asthmatic bat rose above the piano – Emily was still playing.

The man sitting directly in front of her turned round and tried to remove her music. She grabbed it, and a fierce battle began. The music was pulled this way and that until there was the unmistakable sound of tearing paper. This was immediately followed by a loud moan from the second oboe, who happened to double as the librarian.

The audience found all this drama much more interesting than the pianist, and he never really regained their attention. I believe it was the last time he agreed to work with amateurs, and who can blame him.

Bluffers are also likely to disrupt concerts, but they manage to appear innocent while doing so. Some even seem to be making a positive contribution to the music. Read on, and I will reveal some of the secrets of the successful Bluffer, which you should have little difficulty in putting into practice.

Equipment

Pricing Yourself Into The Market

Unless you are a pianist, you will soon tire of playing on your own. You will enjoy yourself much more in an orchestra, so joining one should be your first objective.

Before doing so you will need to provide yourself with some equipment, and even learn to use it.

If you need to buy an instrument, then I am in favour of getting something relatively inexpensive. It is good for your image to be able to give the impression that only reduced circumstances are preventing you from becoming a virtuoso. You will be surprised how much your reputation is enhanced if you say such things as 'This is only a cheap oboe. Some of the cross-fingerings are rather complicated!' But be careful not to make that sort of comment within the hearing of anyone who knows anything about it. Most conductors won't.

For string players, a cheap instrument is a good excuse for producing an indifferent tone. You are going to make a rotten sound anyway, so why not blame it on the fiddle?

Take a good look at the two instruments illustrated on page 13. You will make much the same noise on either of them, but one comes a little cheaper.

A View From The Stands

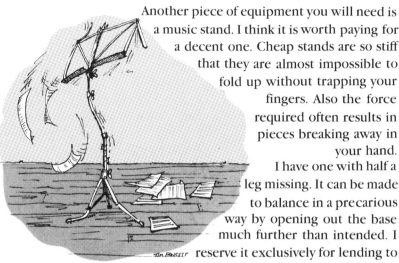

Another piece of equipment you will need is a music stand. I think it is worth paying for a decent one. Cheap stands are so stiff that they are almost impossible to fold up without trapping your fingers. Also the force required often results in pieces breaking away in your hand. I have one with half a leg missing. It can be made to balance in a precarious way by opening out the base much further than intended. I reserve it exclusively for lending to other people, and live in hope that they will return the wrong one. So far I've had no luck.

Some orchestras provide their own stands. Although it saves you the inconvenience of bringing one, it is not much of an advantage. The stands are usually in a poor state of repair, and either droop alarmingly at each side to resemble a CND emblem, or lack vital screws.

If they droop, you will have trouble balancing the music on them. Even if you succeed you are still compelled to play with your head cocked on one side. This is particularly irritating for bassoon and tuba players. They already have enough problems trying to see round the plumbing. Fiddlers have to be contortionists anyway, so it is not such a hardship for them.

When there are screws missing the top of the stand spins round every time you touch the music. It is a pathetic sight to see a musician vainly trying to catch up with his part as he attempts to mark in the con- ductor's latest whim. All the more so as in five minutes the latter will change his mind, and the instruction will have to be rubbed out.

An additional disadvantage of stands with missing screws is that it's impossible to put them up high enough to blot out the conductor. Nothing is more distracting for the players than seeing one of these egotists swaying around with arms flailing as he tries unsuccessfully to keep in time with the orchestra.

If you have some spare cash, there is one luxury item you might get — an extra fiddle case. Choose one that is as light as possible. It doesn't matter about the interior. Normally you will not be putting anything in it, though if you can find a thermos flask and sandwich box that will fit so much the better. It is for use as a prop when attending concerts, particularly violin recitals, and is intended to boost your reputation with other members of the audience.

There is no need for this ploy to be confined to violinists. If you are really a trombone player it doesn't matter. Should you meet a friend, you can easily explain that you are looking after it for someone. Only if your baggage is searched need you fear any potential embarrassment.

Having provided yourself with an instrument the next stage is to use it.

Some years ago I answered an advertisement in a magazine asking for players to form a new orchestra. I decided to give them a try. When we met on the first evening I was one of only three fiddles. Apart from us there were two horns and a clarinet.

Somehow or other we struggled through Schubert's "Unfinished Symphony". The conductor did his best, whistling some of the missing parts. We could at least claim that we added a new dimension to its incompleteness.

The following week the attendance was no better, and when we parted I made some feeble excuse and never returned.

Although few amateur orchestras are as badly cast as that one, it is by no means rare for the string sections to be reduced to a single desk, or not to exist at all. Even when there is a good turnout, half the section won't be playing at any one time.

As a result of these shortages it is seldom difficult for you to get into whichever orchestra you choose. The ability to play at a reasonable standard would appear to be the minimum requirement. And in practice even that is unnecessary. To own an instrument is often sufficient. You may be expected to exaggerate your ability, but you are not likely to be tested.

In rare instances you may be asked to do an audition. Although I have played in at least a dozen orchestras, it has only happened to me once.

Of course it is no use to turn up for an audition and just play badly. You need a convincing tale to arouse the listener's sympathy. Make sure your excuse is implausible, and there is a good chance that it will be believed. When I attended, I said that I had sprained my wrist playing bridge. As someone who has broken an ankle on a putting green I considered it to be a highly convincing story. It is only fair to record that the conductor thought otherwise, and judged me entirely on merit. As a result of this treatment I was rejected.

I learned a couple of years later that, due to lack of support, the orchestra had folded — it won't be missed.

Probably the best policy for string players asked to audition is to apply elsewhere. Life is not so kind if you are a wind player. You will almost always have to audition, and you will be up against plenty of opposition. It means that the true amateur, the person who has maintained the same level of mediocrity for years, stands no real chance.

Go prepared. Don't learn a new piece, but give the impression that you have done so. This is simple. Select a work that you have been playing for a decade, buy a new copy of the music, and take that with you.

It also pays to discover what the orchestra is rehearsing, and get the scores out of the library. Any test is likely to be taken from these. You don't want to find yourself sight reading something that you haven't practised.

Probably the best way of succeeding at any audition is to be female, attractive, and a friend of the conductor. It is not easy to fulfil all these conditions. Some conductors refuse every offer of friendship.

If you consistently fail auditions, you might do well to take up a string instrument. As I have explained, there is no need to reach a stunning level of virtuosity. Once in an orchestra you can keep an eye on the wind section of your choice, and act as a substitute if the regular player fails to turn up.

Item A	**Item B**
Paganini's "Cannon", a fine violin by Guarneri, circa 1742	Akehurst's "Cannon", a general purpose viola of uncertain date

Key to illustration:
1. Accumulation of rosin that the owner has been too lazy to remove, 1978-1986
2. Fingerprints imbedded in varnish. (Possibly due to hot sweaty hands) 1978-1986
3. Nasty crack, which appeared after misjudging speed of a revolving door 1979
4. Real ale stain 1984
5. Evidence of severe chewing, sustained when fending off Norman's dog "Ludwig" 1982
6. Traces of jam (probably gooseberry) circa 1981

Rehearsals
Sowing The Seeds
of Chaos

You are now properly equipped, and have joined a suitable orchestra. The correct way to approach rehearsals is your next concern.

In this country it is common for professional orchestras to suffer from a shortage of rehearsal time. In contrast, amateur orchestras frequently spend far too much time in preparation. It's not unusual for them to have as many as ten meetings before a concert.

Under these circumstances it is a mistake to attend every week. There is a real danger of becoming familiar with the notes, and thus losing the element of surprise so essential to the real enjoyment of playing.

I once took part in a performance of Haydn's "Creation" for which I had not even been able to attend the dress rehearsal. I was thus able to approach the music with a freshness and spontaneity which considerably unnerved the conductor.

I wouldn't really recommend missing all the rehearsals, but it is worth being selective. If you belong to one of those efficiently run groups that issue schedules, you can avoid ever having to work on pieces you don't like. Alternatively, if you are more conscientious, you can arrange to play through the whole programme a limited number of times. Either approach is preferable to rehearsing solidly for three months.

Two objectives should dominate your behaviour within the orchestra. First, when it comes to the concert, you want to be noticed by your friends in the audience. I will deal with this problem in a later section. Second, and this applies as much at rehearsals as in concerts, you must hide your incompetence as a player.

Most of the techniques for obscuring the fact that you simply can't play properly take advantage of the "safety in numbers" principle, and are therefore only applicable to strings.

There are four basic methods:

1. *The Delayed Turn*

One of the simplest ploys is to be the page turner. It is encouraging how many nasty passages occur near the bottom of one page, and at the top of the next. By turning in a careful and methodical manner these can easily be avoided.

I once shared a desk with a lady who applied this system in a particularly exaggerated way, spending a large proportion of the evening leaning forward with her hand outstretched. Unfortunately she was so engrossed in dodging the notes that she frequently forgot to turn the page at all.

2. *Silent Strokes*

Not all the difficult sections are going to fall near the page turn, so it is essential to develop other skills. One of the most widely used is faking. Learn to play really quietly. It is worth working at this, as the rewards are tremendous. If you can reach a sufficiently high standard it doesn't matter what notes you play all evening. But do try to move your bow at the correct speed in order to make it convincing.

Faking is especially useful when you lose your place — one of the most common crises with which you will be faced.

3. *Counterfeit Notes*

The alternative to faking is busking. This can be useful in loud passages, but can be a bit dangerous if you are supposed to be playing quietly. Again it is important to keep your bow moving at the correct speed. If you stick to the basic chord of the home key you should be pretty safe. A few arpeggios usually do the job nicely. I am rashly assuming that you can recognise key signatures. But beware — some composers stoop to underhand tricks like modulating through several keys. It makes busking especially risky.

4. *Division of Labour*

If you are presented with long semiquaver passages, it is sometimes possible to arrange with a sympathetic partner to play alternate bars. This halves the number of notes you have to master, and gives your fingers time to cool down.

In exceptional circumstances you may be reduced to learning the notes, but only resort to this if all else fails. Before doing so, take a look at the full score. There are few things more maddening than learning a difficult passage, only to discover at the concert that it is completely swamped by the brass.

It pays to sit near the back of your section. Apart from the remote danger of being asked to play a solo if the principal goes sick, it is an obvious advantage not to be under the conductor's eye. So long as you keep your voice down you can exchange gossip, or ogle the flute section. (For some reason the flute is an instrument particularly popular with pretty girls. I have never discovered a scientific explanation for this. It is a phenomenon I have learned to live with.) I have seen orchestras where the front desks were deserted, while players competed for space at the back.

As a wind player, with a part to yourself, few of these techniques can be used. You should however be on the look-out for places where you are inaudible, and be ready to use stalling tactics. The most popular gambit, after completely muffing an exposed solo, is to start scraping your reed, or to blow loudly into one of the keys.

I could name a clarinettist who always happens to have his instrument stripped down just when he reaches a tricky section.

There is one other problem you will meet whatever your instrument — learning to be silent when you are not supposed to be playing. I don't know why some people have so much difficulty with rests. Counting is one of the few things I can do at all well.

At one time I shared a stand with a lady who could not. Ever certain that she was right, she used to come in with such confidence at the wrong place that I frequently followed her.

Of course some players make no effort to count at all, but rely on their partners. I have developed a couple of childish tricks to play on them. These help to while away the time when you have a long wait, so try them for yourself.

If, for example, you have about 30 bars rest, delay for 20 or so and then pick up your instrument and put the bow ready on the string. Your partner will almost certainly do the same — at which point of course you put it back on your knee. But don't forget to keep on counting.

There is an effective counter measure. Your companion has only to ignore you and the tables are turned, so don't try it more than once per session.

The reverse trick is to sit back and look carelessly around the room. When there is about a beat and a half to go you should leap into action, just managing to come in on time. There is no real counter to this one.

The Conductor
Drifting With The Wind

In addition to knowing what to do about the music, you must also know how to handle the conductor. He will be doing his best to thwart any signs of individuality in the musicians. For instance a girl studying percussion came to a rehearsal, bringing a large suitcase with her. Inside was an impressive array of specialist equipment. There were drumsticks with hard heads and drumsticks with soft heads. There were gourds filled with gravel that rattled charmingly when they were shaken. There was a fine collection of small bells, strung together like French onions. To crown it all, there was a mysterious object that closely resembled a loofah. (Perhaps she sometimes practised in the bath.)

All these implements she carefully laid out in neat rows on a table near the timps. She might have been a surgeon preparing for an operation.

The conductor's response was simple. He confined her activities to a few blows on the triangle.

Sometimes, during loud passages, the conductor may get excited and start to accelerate. Should this happen, it is a mistake to try and follow him. Not only does it call for greater dexterity than you are likely to possess, but it is the orchestra's duty to keep a steady tempo which the conductor can follow without too much effort.

One conductor for whom I played got so worked up that he managed to stab himself in the eye with his baton, fortunately with no serious consequences.

(Incidentally, when a conductor throws his baton over his shoulder into the audience near the end of a concert, or snaps it against the desk, you can be sure it is a well rehearsed manœuvre. Any incident of that sort which happens under genuine circumstances will occur early on, when he still needs it to conduct.)

Some conductors waste a great deal of rehearsal time on unnecessary detail. I remember one who spent half an hour getting a beautiful double hairpin on the last chord of a major romantic symphony. However when it came to the concert most of the musicians were lost long before the end, and the whole exercise was futile.

What conductors should do is to agree on a few simple signals so that they can indicate where they have got to. It should be possible to devise something more subtle than to shout out a letter in a loud voice.

You may come across conductors who make life unnecessarily difficult. If they want to begin half way through a movement, they have a habit of counting out loud without giving you any reference point. Having reached the place where they want to start they are then surprised that you are no longer with them.

Remember that an amateur orchestra also serves as a social club. The fact that a rehearsal is in progress should in no way discourage you from chatting to your neighbour. It is sensible to establish the relationships between players at an early stage. It can be a little disconcerting to criticise the conductor, and then to find that you are talking to his wife.

Don't take too seriously the sort of conductor who says 'This is not a drinking orchestra'. He is unlikely to be right. If you want to end the evening in the pub, you will find plenty of takers in the wind and brass sections. (A glance at the floor by their feet will indicate how much liquid they need to replace.)

One conductor I knew liked to think of his orchestra as a sort of marriage bureau. Treat such situations with caution. It is as well to bear in mind that if things go wrong at least one of you will have to resign.

It is not often that an amateur orchestra is pressed into giving an encore. Most audiences have heard more than enough by the interval, never mind when the concert has staggered to its conclusion. However I did once take part in a performance where the same piece was played twice. The conductor was of the opinion that the programme was too short. No amateur concert is ever too short. On this occasion the audience was astonished to read in the programme that Mozart's "Masonic Funeral Music" was to be played twice by way of an overture. Any lingering hope they may have had that there was some colossal misprint was dispelled as we started the piece for the second time.

There was no repeat of the applause — the audience was taking no chances on the work being encored. Just occasionally a conductor may come up with a good idea. Understandably most amateur concerts are poorly attended, but one man hit upon a novel method to create the illusion of a high turnout. The concert in question took place in a town hall, where the seating consisted of those canvas and steel chairs popular about 20 years ago — the sort that leave red weals on your thighs after about seven minutes. Anyway this conductor simply stacked up the first 15 rows to leave a blank area the size of a tennis court between orchestra and audience. The supporters were thus concentrated in the relatively few remaining seats, and it was even possible to put up a 'Full House' notice and turn a couple of people away. It is the only occasion when I can remember there being adequate space for the musicians.

Haydn
The Finishing Touches

At this point, let us look at how a typical rehearsal might go. It is supposed to start at 7.30, but by 7.25 only three people have turned up. They are all pensioners from the back desks of the second fiddles, and they have been there for at least a quarter of an hour. During that time they have put out most of the chairs. These are about 11 inches high, the rehearsal being held in an infants school. Fortunately they are designed to be stacked. By using two, most people will be able to sit as much as 15 inches above the ground. The cellos will need four chairs each. This will give them a disturbing sense of instability, and at least one may find himself unseated before the evening is over.

At this point the principal flute arrives. He is a middle-aged civil servant, and chairman of the orchestra. He looks around disapprovingly at the poor attendance, unlocks a cupboard, and starts putting up stands.

A View From The Stands

He lacks any sort of mechanical sense, and several of them, already in less than perfect condition, will be further distorted by his efforts. More people are now starting to appear, and by 7.45 even the conductor has arrived.

At ten minutes to eight the players have settled down in their seats, and are making an appalling row as they warm up. If you look round you may spot a few differences from a professional band.

The second violins outnumber the firsts by about two to one, and their aggregate ages by about five to one. There are only two violas and three cellos.

There is a solitary bass player — one more than usual. He is really a jazz freak, and misses a high proportion of rehearsals to play in gigs. He tends to play pizzicato much more frequently than is called for in the score.

The first oboe is a sixth-former. She got into the orchestra because she is at school with the conductor's daughter.

The second is an old man and past his prime. He is allowed to stay on as a reward for long service.

The second flute, a girl in her twenties, though not brilliant is better than the first. There is an element of friction between them, and they seldom exchange a word.

The first clarinet doubles as the orchestra clown, and is capable of incapacitating the entire wind section with a couple of words. He is a good player, but suffers from nerves. Neither clarinet is present this evening.

There is only one bassoon player, a relative beginner. At the concert he will be expected to take the second part, and an extra will be brought in to play first.

The horn section is also a one man outfit. Recruited from a brass band, his first instrument is the euphonium. He is easily perplexed by the various transpositions that his part calls for. As horns are difficult to find, his place is secure, but he will get some coaching from the conductor before the performance. As the latter is a keyboard player, this instruction will produce no marked improvement.

The horn player has some undefined relationship with the second flute. He thinks it is a secret between the two of them but in fact it is a matter of intense speculation throughout the orchestra.

There are no regular trumpets, trombones or tubas, and extras will be required to fill these positions at concerts.

At 7.47 the conductor calls for silence and asks for an A. The oboist is trying out a new reed, and the A is about a semi-tone sharp. There are cries of 'sharp' (and a few of 'flat') from around the orchestra, and then everyone gives his own version as loudly as possible. The discord continues for about a minute. No-one makes any attempt to correct the pitch of his instrument, although there is a span of nearly a tone across the board.

Eventually, during a lull, the conductor indicates that he wants to run through the symphony. It is No. 94 by Haydn — "The Surprise".

At this moment the chairman rises to his feet and announces that he has something to say. He never misses a chance to make a speech. If he gets his way he will mount the rostrum. He now delivers a fierce attack on those who arrived late. As this means most of the orchestra, no-one is much concerned. There is a little ironic clapping when at last he sits down, and the conductor then raises his baton to start. It is now three minutes to eight.

The symphony opens with a short Adagio. Initially the scoring is for oboes, bassoons and horns. As only four of the six parts are represented, the sound is significantly thinner than that envisaged by Haydn. It is further impaired by the contribution from the horn player.

His part is written in G, but either he can only cope with horn parts in F, or hasn't checked the music. At any rate he injects a D instead of the written E. It does little to improve the harmony.

As this is supposed to be a run through, and the conductor doesn't want to hold things up more than necessary, he waves play on, and the band staggers along to the end of the Adagio.

At this point he raises his hands to indicate a brief pause before the Vivace. Unfortunately not all the players are watching him. In fact only about three are, and a majority carry on playing. Such chaos results that the Vivace has to be restarted.

A View From The Stands

At the second attempt the violins get away to a reasonable start. Not so the violas, who join in half a bar behind. As they are playing repeated notes, it takes a number of bars for the mistake to show up. By that stage the reason for it has become obscure.

The orchestra manages to keep more or less together until they reach bar 58. Then the first fiddles, confronted by a semi-quaver passage generously sprinkled with accidentals, collapse in confusion.

The conductor decides that once again he cannot let it pass. He takes them three times through the notes at a much reduced tempo, and then tries it up to speed. No improvement can be detected. The rest of the players soon tire of this sort of thing, and start talking among themselves. Newspapers appear, and sweets are passed round.

The first movement ends without further incident, and a start is made on the Andante — the movement with the surprise chord from which the symphony takes its name. If you believe that the chord is so predictable as to be no surprise at all, you would take heart from this rehearsal, as the second violins manage to play it a beat before everyone else. They are rewarded with a look of pity from the conductor, and hoots of derision from the other players.

Next the minor section is reached. At this watershed, two of the senior second fiddles leave their places and go into the pantry to put the kettle on. It is a little on the early side for the interval, but they have spotted a couple of lines approaching which look ominously black. Timing the coffee break is principally a matter of tactics.

About four minutes later the orchestra stops for the interval. The rehearsal has been under way scarcely half an hour, but coffee takes precedence over everything else. The chairman gets in a couple of words about keeping the break to a minimum. They fall on deaf ears.

It is a good 30 minutes before anyone goes back to his place. The Andante has yet to be completed, and the minor section proves to be a stumbling block not only for the strings, but also for the inexperienced bassoonist. Unable to cope with it, he agrees to look at it at home. He will do no such thing.

The Minuet is sufficiently straight forward to be played through without a break, and the band starts the Finale believing that they are almost good enough to appear on the South Bank. However the first violins are soon in difficulties, and have to be taken through it again on their own.

It is now well into injury time, and one or two members have started to pack up their instruments and sneak out on tiptoe. It is only the school caretaker, pointedly standing in the doorway rattling his keys and letting in a cold blast of air, who finally brings the evening to a close.

Next week the conductor will select another work from the concert programme. The results will be much the same, and in the mean time the orchestra will forget everything about the Haydn. When next it appears on the stands it will seem once more like sight-reading.

Early in the season you will probably be told the date of the Annual General Meeting. It is important to put it in your diary at once. It may take some time to organise a previous engagement. I always feel safer if I can be out of the country, but it is not really necessary to go to that much trouble.

The A.G.M. follows the same dreary and predictable pattern every year. First the secretary reads out the minutes of the last meeting. They are unanimously approved. It comes as no great surprise, since few members are likely to recall what was said last year.

After the minutes comes the high water-mark of the evening – the chairman's speech. In it he details the achievements of the orchestra over the last 12 months. As the orchestra will not have achieved anything in that time, or indeed for the last ten years, what he says will be mostly fiction.

Members who have had the foresight to sit near the back will find this an excellent opportunity to finish the crossword. Those at the front must content themselves with the thought that the speech will probably be shorter than Rheingold. On the negative side there will be no Rhine Maidens to liven things up.

Next comes the treasurer's report. It is accompanied by a balance sheet, incomprehensible to all, which shows the orchestra as usual in debt. The report includes proposals for raising money. They all amount to a whip round, and a vote is duly taken. For some reason, no-one ever objects on these occasions.

The final business of the meeting is the election of committee members. It is on this account that you should arrange alternative engagements. I have known cases where people have been elected to office in their absence, but the danger is much greater when you are visible.

If you are tempted to get yourself voted onto the committee in the hope of having some influence on the choice of future works, you are deluding yourself. All music is chosen by the chairman — with the tacit approval of the conductor. Selecting programmes is his special privilege and he won't give you a look-in. He is ever on the watch for pieces which provide him with jammy solos.

In practice this is not as bad as it sounds, because there is a limit to the number of works that give preference to any one instrument. You can take some satisfaction from the fact that he will probably fluff his solos anyway.

The Dress Rehearsal
A Foretaste of Disaster

About halfway through the rehearsal schedule a member of the committee, who has been delegated to sell tickets, will attempt to corner you. This unhappy individual is not sure if he has contracted some contagious disease. Almost anyone he approaches dashes across the room and starts an earnest conversation with someone else.

If he eventually pins you down, make sure that you have come to rehearsal without any money. It's an oversight you may well repeat the next week.

The ticket seller's only hope is to persuade people to take a few on a sale or return basis. This looks a good move until the day of the concert, when he is snowed under with unsold returns.

Do not be intimidated by the type of conductor who insists that everyone must sell ten tickets. He won't throw you out if you fail. If he did, there would be no players left at all. Don't get into a discussion on the subject. Just nod in agreement and buy your regular two.

Having got the tickets you then have to decide what to do with them. I find that they take up very little room at the bottom of a wastepaper basket.

Once or twice I have given them to friends — I have never had the audacity to charge for them. The problem is to find people who are more or less indifferent to music. Those who care about it don't want to hear it ruined; those who don't are hardly likely to turn up. Any who come can usually be persuaded that they have had a pleasant evening. On average this takes between three and four pints. A minority have remained friendly after the ordeal. No-one has come a second time.

There is one sort of friend to whom you should never offer tickets — other amateur musicians. They will only retaliate by inviting you to their concerts.

If the concert is to take place in a church, you may be pressed into service the previous evening to set the stage. This is another of those dates when a previous engagement can prove invaluable.

If you agree to lend a hand it is most important to arrive late. That way most of the heavy work, like shifting pews, should already have been done.

Make sure that everyone knows that you suffer from vertigo. Some mug is going to find himself 20 feet up a ladder, swinging like a monkey from the rafters as he adjusts the lighting. Take care it isn't you.

Make the most of being there by ensuring that your section has enough chairs and stands, and that some of the lights are directed towards them. The bulbs will undoubtedly blow during the concert, but you might as well get a glimpse of your part first.

Most amateur concerts take place on Saturday evenings, so the Dress Rehearsal is normally held in the afternoon. This is a serious blow for sports fans.

If the rehearsal interferes with sport, it is also true that sport will disrupt the rehearsal. You will find that concert promoters think nothing else is going on in town. If the concert takes place in Twickenham, it is bound to coincide with a rugby international. If it is in Wembley it will be on Cup Final day; if in Wimbledon the tennis will be in full swing. The result is that you will be stuck in a traffic jam for three quarters of an hour, and then there will be nowhere to park.

Eventually you may find a space close to one of those yellow cones that the police so thoughtfully place on pavements to trip unwary pedestrians. After the rehearsal, when you have only 90 minutes to dash home, grab a meal, and change, your car will be waiting for you in a police pound ten miles away. You certainly won't have time to collect it before Sunday.

In practice you might as well arrive a little late for Dress Rehearsals. They never start on time, so why hang around getting cold for nothing? But although I advocate being a little late, it is a mistake to arrive after play has begun. Even if a chair has been kept for you, it will probably have drifted into another section, where it will be serving as a table for a couple of handbags. It's remarkable how many people you can disrupt by grabbing your chair and sitting down.

It is a fact of life that there is never quite enough room for the orchestra to sit comfortably. It means that you are frequently putting your elbow into someone's ribs, or having your specs knocked off by some flamboyant bowing. The last desk of first violins may be concealed behind the pulpit. (If the right players are delegated to this position it can only enhance the performance.)

In order to move your arm at all it may be necessary to sit sideways on. This is really an advantage, because you won't be able to see the conductor. As things start to go wrong at a performance the expression, at first of alarm and later of panic, which spreads across his face will be communicated to anyone who happens to look at him. They in turn will make an increasing number of errors. Scientists describe this phenomenon as positive feedback. There are more colloquial phrases for it, which I won't go into here.

Dress Rehearsals take place in sub-zero temperatures, irrespective of the season. Why churches are always so cold I have no idea. Musicians have enough problems with the notes without the added difficulties of frozen fingers. But don't make the mistake of putting on extra layers under your dress clothes when you go home to change. On returning, it is quite likely that someone will have switched on a hitherto undiscovered heating system of remarkable efficiency. The church will have been transformed into something resembling the palm house at Kew, and you will be drenched in perspiration throughout the concert.

It is at the Dress Rehearsal that the extras first make their appearance. They add to the chaos, especially if the strings are being reinforced. Now it is discovered that there are insufficient parts. Naturally no-one will have told the librarian how many extras are coming, and he certainly won't have thought of asking. It means that some of you will be sitting three to a desk.

(The librarian, incidently, has one of the most thankless tasks in the orchestra. Not only is he held responsible for all the parts that go missing, but is expected to carry a heavy suitcase full of music around. Don't offer to help – you may end up with his job.)

The greatest influx of extras is normally in the brass. It is common for the entire section to be making its debut at the Dress Rehearsal. Usually composed of a vociferous bunch of students, watch them for hints on how to irritate conductors.

Don't be disappointed if they fail to obliterate all your difficult bits during the rehearsal. They will play much louder at the concert.

Some continental orchestras reverse the position of the viola and cello sections. It is a policy that I strongly favour, and it's well worth try-

ing to convince the conductor of the acoustic benefits. Of course it doesn't really make the remotest difference to the sound, but it does get you away from the trumpets.

The cellos will naturally resist any such switch. They don't like being deafened either, and are used to being out of the conductor's immediate line of vision and able to chatter during rehearsals. Don't attempt to wear ear-muffs, as you will certainly be made to take them off. However a little cotton wool stuffed into each ear can usually be explained away on medical grounds.

By the time the concerto is rehearsed the soloist will be fuming. Having arrived as requested at three o'clock, she has been compelled to sit through an extra half hour devoted to the overture. It has given her a revealing insight into just how much support she can expect from the orchestra. The chairman will probably aggravate the situation further by calling for a break between works, and keep her waiting even longer. The wise conductor will not have invited her to a previous rehearsal. Given sufficient warning, she may well be "indisposed" for the concert.

You will find that Dress Rehearsals always overrun the predicted finishing time. There is no need to stay to the end. It is more important to have a proper meal. Allowing yourself an insufficient break before the concert will spoil your performance.

When you return to the 'Green Room' before the concert you will be surrounded by exhibitionists wandering about in a random fashion playing extracts from concertos. None of them can play more than about eight bars, but they will repeat them remorselessly. Have nothing to do with this sort of behaviour. Use the time to prepare yourself properly for the concert. For example, check that your sweets are wrapped in something that doesn't crackle when you open them, and that you have paper and pencil to draw caricatures of the soloist during lengthy and tedious cadenzas.

If you sit out a whole movement, as sometimes happens to wind players, a novel could be useful. A book of cartoons is, however, a mistake. Conductors do not take kindly to players who burst out laughing during performances.

The Concert
Your Worst Fears Realised

Don't expect the evening to start with the music. Although the audience's patience is tried enough by the scheduled programme, many concerts begin with a speech.

I remember a lady from the local evening institute who insisted on telling the audience about everything that was going to happen in the borough. We had bets in the violas as to how long she would drone on. Our guesses were all too low.

One conductor I played for liked to introduce each work with a few well chosen words, most often some improbable quotations from the composer. Actually I think he made most of them up, or perhaps they suffered badly in translation. One day, to the delight of those listening, he introduced a piece as 'Bolero's Ravel'. After that he seemed more reluctant to speak. There were a couple of occasions when he invited a friend along to do the talking. However this chap spoke at such length that he threatened to take over the performance, and was quickly given the boot.

When it comes to the concert don't forget your two priorities — being noticed by your friends, but concealing your inability to play most of the notes.

One simple method of standing out is through your clothes. For instance tradition calls for a black bow tie and a dinner jacket. I like to wear a velvet jacket and a plum-coloured bow tie. For the ladies, a low cut dress (if you have the figure for it) has the double advantage of mak-

A View From The Stands

ing you stand out, and taking attention away from what your fingers are doing. Or not doing.

You can also capitalise on the way you use your instrument. If a string player, you could develop a prominent vibrato. It does nothing to improve your tone, but it does inspire respect in the audience. If a wind player, wave the bell of your instrument in an exaggerated way, or raise and lower your elbows as you breathe. But be sure to keep in time with the music.

Don't forget that the concert is entirely for the benefit of the players, so enjoy yourself. Dynamics are only marked into the parts to spoil rehearsals. There is a simple rule for playing in concerts. Play the easy bits loud and ease off when the going gets tough. You won't be thrown out of the band. They need your subscription. Anyway the conductor has plenty of other things to worry about, and is unlikely to notice.

Don't concern yourself about what the audience thinks. They are not going to enjoy it anyway, and few of them will bother to check the score. Most are counting off the minutes before they can sneak out for a smoke.

There are a number of hazards which may disrupt your concert. First, birds. On one occasion a pigeon got into the church shortly after a concert began. About every ten minutes, just as everyone had forgotten about it, there would be a clatter of wings as it selected a new perch. Occasionally, by way of a diversion, it beat against a window for a couple of seconds before returning to a vantage point above the orchestra. I need hardly say that the sight of a pigeon sitting on a rafter immediately overhead did nothing to improve our concentration, and we were all relieved when someone assisted it to escape during the interval.

Some works call for a player, or even a small band, to be positioned off-stage. This sort of thing is risky. For example, much careful planning can be ruined at a stroke if an intervening door blows shut. (I would happily see the brass permanently removed from the platform, where they can't frighten away innocent old ladies at the back of the second fiddles. But few conductors seem to agree with me.)

A common problem in churches is striking clocks. They invariably chime in the bits marked pianissimo, just when the orchestra has built up a sense of mystery and tension, and the audience are on the edges of their seats in breathless anticipation. (You may detect a note of irony here. No amateur orchestra can play below mezzo-forte anyway, and the audience will be slumped back in their chairs, glancing furtively at their watches.) For this reason, perhaps, the tradition of beginning concerts a little after the hour has something to recommend it.

Most church clocks can be disabled with a couple of strategically placed six inch nails, though it is not always simple to get into the belfry. If you succeed, don't forget to remove them after the concert. You don't

Man looking for mute

JIM FAWCETT

want the repair bill to be sent to the orchestra, and the inevitable witch-hunt that will follow.

Dropping bits of equipment is another common distraction. I remember at one performance a trumpeter failed to insert his mute properly. During a quiet passage it clattered onto the floor, then rolled down amongst the strings. As the owner was imprisoned behind a wall of stands, one of the horn players went in search of it. The back desks of fiddles were rather surprised to see a man crawling around on his hands and knees at their feet in the middle of a concert, but they pretended it was nothing unusual. Eventually he retrieved the mute, and returned it with a cry of triumph. The triumph was short-lived, because he immediately missed an important entry.

Sometimes it is possible to have only one note to play, and yet to upstage the whole orchestra. I saw this perfected by a percussion player.

The man was plump, bald and bespectacled. It was hard to accept that he was a real person, and not the incarnation of a Hoffnung drawing. About five minutes before he had anything to do he rose to his feet and collected a triangle. He then stood perfectly to attention and held it before him at arms' length. After a couple of minutes he lifted his left leg clear of the ground, pushing it out to one side and keeping the knee straight. He then replaced it on the floor and went through exactly the same routine with the right leg. All this time he kept his little piece of bent wire raised in readiness before him.

While this was going on the 90 remaining musicians on the platform built the music up towards its climax. But their efforts went unregarded by the audience. All eyes remained fixed on the solitary figure of the percussionist.

After what seemed a great age his moment arrived. He struck a single blow and retired to his seat. I wish I could claim that he missed his cue, but he came in right on time.

I rather thought the conductor might get him up to take a bow at the end. It would have been a popular decision. However they do not take kindly to anything that smacks of competition, and he had to remain seated.

You should keep a look-out for a reporter from the local paper. I suppose it must be difficult to fill 20 pages every week with provincial news, and a crit. makes easy copy.

The chances are that the reporter will know little, and care less, about the music. It is the duty of a committee member to identify this person, and see that his evening ends on a pleasant note in the pub. That way the band should be able to get a decent write-up.

If you are unfortunate enough to be sent someone who knows about music, getting a satisfactory report could prove more tricky. However make him welcome just the same. He may come to a compromise where he damns the performance in such a pretentious and ambiguous manner that it almost seems like praise. He may even be so taken up with producing something of literary merit that he forgets some of the more glaring errors in the concert.

Below are a few examples of disguised insults that might appear in a concert report, together with their true meanings.

Quote   The acoustic ambience, far from blending the timbre of the individual instruments, made them shimmer with independent vitality.

Meaning There was a total lack of ensemble.

Quote   Unhurried tempi and sonorous cantabile gave the symphony an air of benign tranquility.

Meaning The symphony was played so slowly that I fell asleep from unrelieved boredom.

Quote   There was an invigorating freedom from routine that characterised this unconventional interpretation.

Meaning The performance bore little or no resemblance to the written music.

Quote   Some ragged moments in the higher passages of the violin part were rare blemishes in a performance demonstrating remarkable technique.

Meaning The violins were out of tune most of the time.

Quote   We were presented with a succession of shapes and colours that held us spellbound in this transparent interpretation.

Meaning The conductor was not in control of the orchestra.

A View From The Stands

The great advantage of such writing is that you are entitled to read all sorts of extravagant compliments into it, and should not be disheartened from trying again next time. It can also be gratifying for the conductor (whose sole ambition had been to keep the orchestra more or less together, and at least to start and finish at the same time) to read that he 'never lost sight of the music's thematic unity, while emphasising the dynamic contrast between the first and second subjects'.

The Inside Story

Playing Away From Home

Sometimes orchestras are asked to give concerts in prisons. These are the only times you are likely to play to a full house. As classical music is unlikely to be popular with many prisoners, I presume attendance must be compulsory. Perhaps it is an extension of the penal system?

Remember these audiences do not always react to the music, but will certainly respond to you. On one occasion, a girl turned up in a backless dress that would have caused a sensation in a nightclub. She was not the sort of woman who shuns publicity, but I think even she was a little taken aback by the whistling she provoked.

However this response was dwarfed by the uproar that greeted Alice. At that time short skirts were in fashion, and Alice was wearing one. That would not have been so significant were she not a lady in her fifties, and built like a Japanese wrestler. As it was, she shuffled through the band to her seat at the front of the strings accompanied by cheers and stamping on a massive scale.

As I lived close to her, I used to take Alice to rehearsals. In those days I had a small convertible car, and in order to accommodate both of us and

TIM FAWCETT

her cello it was necessary to drive with the hood down. The inhabitants of Bromley were thus treated to the bizarre spectacle of two eccentric motorists and a cello braving the winter rain in an open car, with one side about six inches closer to the road than the other. As we crawled up Crystal Palace hill in low gear one day, she told me that in her youth she had often cycled up it. 'But in those days I only weighed 18 stone', she added.

I was relieved when later I moved to another part of London, and was no longer obliged to take her. It was too late by then to save the car though. It developed a terminal sag in the middle, and had to be put down.

A word of warning on the subject of prison concerts. Don't turn up wearing one of those denim suits fashionable among the young, and would-be young. You may have trouble persuading the authorities to let you out again. And don't make a dramatic appearance with your own ball and chain. Warders have a limited sense of humour.

A few brave orchestras attempt to stage concerts in public parks. This creates a different set of problems. The obvious hazard is the weather. Since such events are usually scheduled for the summer, they have an uncanny knack of coinciding with thunder storms. As the rain lashes down on your instruments there will inevitably be a stampede to the back of the bandstand, and the resulting crush will make further play impossible.

I remember playing in a park to an audience numbering only three. They were all huddled for shelter under a tree about a hundred yards away. At least they had the advantage of being out of earshot of the music. One of the three was a friend of mine. He has now stopped speaking to me.

There are usually enough dogs around to maintain a running battle close by, and all bandstands seem to be directly under a major flight path.

If you do a concert that is nowhere near an airport, then half a dozen lads with unsilenced motorbikes will choose an adjacent road to tune up their engines.

Of course one of the traditional problems for musicians playing in the open air is how to stop the parts blowing away. The normal practice is to use clothes pegs. But if the wind is at all strong — and it always is — it will snatch your music just the same. A few fragments of paper may be left pinned to the stand, but they won't help you much. They will, however, incur the wrath of the librarian, who spends the week after one of these events with an enormous roll of cellotape, trying desperately to piece together the parts. Librarians need an early background in solving jigsaw puzzles.

A View From The Stands

Not only do clothes pegs fail to secure the music properly, they also create almost insurmountable difficulties when the page has to be turned. Holding your instrument, releasing the page at one side, and securing it again at the other — all without losing a grip on the later pages — is quite a feat even in still air. (Experiments using weights suspended from pieces of string do not, in my experience, fare any better.)

If you join an orchestra that makes trips abroad, at least you may get subsidised holidays. Although concerts held in unfamiliar surroundings are often even more hazardous than those on home territory, there are plenty of compensations. You can expect to meet with some generous hospitality, and sometimes gain new friends.

If you are travelling by air, make sure that you take your instrument with you in the passenger compartment. You don't want to let the baggage handlers near it. It's better to spend the flight with a fiddle in your lap than to have to rebuild it when you arrive. That is if it does arrive. One viola player on a trip to Switzerland had to wait for three days while his luggage made a world tour.

Of course the stewardesses don't take too kindly to instrument cases being deposited in the gangway. Officially they constitute a safety hazard, but really they interfere with the profitable business of selling duty-frees. However, if your party occupies most of the plane, the hostesses can be intimidated by sheer numbers, and may relent.

Orchestras on tour seem to lack not only preparation but also players. On a visit to Belgium we arrived with no cellos, and had to borrow a whole section from the local band. As they showed the rest of us up, we were careful to bring our own next time.

Bass players usually have to borrow instruments, since it is obviously not practical to carry them in the plane. Just locating one can be a major headache, and you will be very lucky to find it in playable condition.

Foreign tours produce some original concert settings. On one occasion we played in a large cave. Admittedly it had been converted into a sort of theatre, so conditions were not as primitive as you might imagine.

The problem with caves is that water drips from the roof, and we spent a good deal of valuable rehearsal time wiping the moisture from our instruments rather than preparing for the performance. After a while we worked out where the drips would land, so that by the concert we had reorganised ourselves to avoid them. This produced a bizarre distribution of players, with groups of musicians huddled closely together, and large areas of deserted platform. The drips, of course, fell elsewhere on the night.

This concert ended with a performance of the 1812 overture. It struck me as being a dangerous choice. I had visions of the maroons starting a rock-fall, and players and spectators being buried alive.

In practice all that happened was that there was a colossal amount of smoke, and the orchestra vanished into well-deserved obscurity.

Tours abroad are the only time when it is acceptable to give an encore. In fact encores are almost obligatory. It is a good policy to choose something English. A 'Pomp and Circumstance' march for example. Of course continental audiences do not really like Elgar, and it would be thoughtless to include any in the main programme. However they are quite indulgent about letting the orchestra have a bit of fun, provided it doesn't continue for too long. They are tolerant because the encore will shortly be followed by drinks. This makes them far less critical — unless you are foolish enough to try and subject them to a second encore.

Some conductors choose a piece written in the host country. This can be a mistake, as the average continental audience tends to resent its own music being abused by a foreign orchestra.

Chamber Music 1
Moving Into
The Small Time

If you fancy a change from orchestral playing, why not have a go at chamber music. You don't need to worry about auditions, and you won't have to pay a subscription. But you will need to give careful thought when choosing who to play with. After all, you don't want to spend all evening arguing about politics, or discussing home-made wine.

It may be worth joining an orchestra, even for a short time, just to poach the players you need. If you're forming a string quartet and need a leader, don't assume that everyone in the first fiddles is a potential candidate. Some are there as a long service reward, or only because they are on the committee.

You should definitely try to avoid the know-alls — the ones who seem to be more familiar with your part than their own. They have no scruples about stopping the music and informing on you every time you leave out a couple of tricky notes.

I have a strong preference for away matches, and seldom turn down invitations to play chamber music if there is dinner on offer. It is extraordinary the effect that a few drinks can have in mellowing your criticism of other players. If the music promises to be unusually dull, I am even prepared to help wash up to delay the restart.

Although I have no scruples where food is concerned, I consider it hazardous to mix music and sex.

For example, I have a friend with whom I have spent many happy hours playing chamber music. On one occasion she invited me to join a quintet she was organising. She is one of those people who regard match-making as an amusing hobby, and her motive for starting this particular group was to fix up one of her friends.

She must have been hard up for choice at that time, because it so happened that I was the intended target. Of course I was unaware of that when she asked me, and I suspect her friend was too. However I accepted happily enough. By chance I was attracted to another member of the quintet, thus giving an unexpected twist to the plot.

These meetings continued for several months, without either intrigue succeeding. Looking back it seems unfair that the cellist, an innocent bystander, found himself acting as host for most of the sessions.

When your group meets, the first thing you will notice is some indecision about what to play. This state of affairs can often hold things up for about ten minutes while there is a sort of auction. Everyone has works in mind which he wishes to avoid, and quotes a long list of preferred pieces to be left until next time. The final choice is thus a compromise that pleases nobody.

Occasionally you may arrive to find that the host has already put out the parts. This is always bad news. It means he has selected something that flatters his instrument and it probably means he has practised it. (He will certainly deny having done so.) Be particularly on your guard if music has been put out by the quartet leader. Only he would consider buying Book IV of Haydn quartets. This is a collection that has been specially selected for the unparalleled dullness of the inside parts. Under the conventional auction it is almost impossible to get them played.

One way of dealing with Haydn Book IV is to get one part muddled with your own music. (With only three parts the quartets can't be played.) At home you can dispose of it at your leisure. Take someone else's part though. You don't want suspicion directed at you. The wise second fiddle will have three or four viola and cello copies concealed safely in a bottom draw.

Ideally, once a piece has been chosen, you should claim to be sight reading, even if you have played it five times in the last three months. At least say you haven't seen it for a very long time.

At this stage you will be confronted by another crisis — how to get started. It should be easy enough for the leader to bring in the others with a suitable signal — such as a toss of the head. But in practice this doesn't always work, and you may decide to settle for counting a bar in. Even such crude methods are by no means foolproof, because many leaders count at one speed and start at another.

One of the principal tasks facing you is to fathom out just where the others have got to. If you stop every time you part company, you won't reach the end of anything. Flexibility, coupled with a readiness to shout loudly, are essential qualities. You must be ready to add or drop bars as required. The first to reach a landmark, such as a letter or double bar, should give a clear call. The others can then rally round.

I know one lady who bobs up out of her seat every time she reaches a letter, thus saving her voice for the interval. I recommend this approach if you are not normally more than one letter adrift.

If you keep breaking down at an early stage in a work, it's not a bad idea to check that everyone is playing the same music. This is not as stupid as it sounds. I recall an occasion when repeated attempts to start the Mozart clarinet quintet all ended in failure. The mystery was eventually solved by the second fiddle.

'Just to clear up a point' he said, 'we are playing the Brahms aren't we?'

Sometimes the publisher can cause confusion, particularly if not everyone is playing from the same edition. I have come across cases where movements are not printed in the same order. Also, some volumes of music have alternative numbering systems, so that although everyone is playing say quartet No. 29, one of you is looking at a totally different piece. If you are really unlucky they could even be in the same key.

One thing you will notice is that no-one ever believes he has made a mistake. When a quartet collapses, someone may admit that he went wrong. But this is merely his way of saying that whoever got lost it certainly wasn't him. He is waiting to be contradicted. If you were to agree with him he would probably get up and walk out. However, most players understand the system. After a short discussion it will be concluded that the composer was to blame. Everyone is now exonerated, and the music can continue.

Most of your fellow players give themselves the benefit of the doubt for as long as possible. When it is eventually beyond dispute that they are not together, they do not immediately stop and put things right. Each one believing that it is the others who have lost touch with him, starts to play louder. He is trying to let them know where he has got to. It is a waste of effort, because the others play louder as well, and there is a magnificent crescendo. Eventually everyone collapses from exhaustion.

Some people allow their pets to wander round the room while you are trying to play. It is quite difficult to concentrate on the music if a cat is sharpening its claws on your leg, or a dog is playfully chewing your foot. Should you have friends who are animal lovers, be sure to let them know that you suffer from asthma, and kick the brutes out before any serious injuries occur.

A View From The Stands

Of course a few people really do have asthma. A cellist friend of mine was asked to play in a room recently occupied by a cat. After half an hour he came out in a ghastly scarlet rash, and had to go home. It was a double blow for him, as he had planned to stay the night with the hostess.

I know a wind player whose dog barks whenever she practices. This lady has a theory that the dog is musical, and is showing appreciation. Some people are remarkably naive.

Children are just as much of a menace as animals. They are almost as likely to scratch your ankle, though they usually settle for screaming. They can be as strident and as unmusical as any quartet, and can sustain a fortissimo for much longer.

Unfortunately the only short-term solution that doesn't result in criminal proceedings is to give them attention. It is a pitiful sight to see a father trying to lead a quartet, while a child sits on his knee and tries to strangle him with his own tie. It is not uncommon.

It's a good policy to keep a can of beer within reach. Then you can have a swig whenever there are several bars rest to count. If there is a long break, resist the temptation to go out of the room and make a mug of coffee. It gives the other players an uneasy feeling that all is not quite as it should be, and the music is sure to break down. Rather, use the time to work out which notes you are going to leave out in the next tricky section.

You will quickly realise that every second fiddle player has an urge to upstage the other members of the quartet. He feels an overwhelming desire to prove himself, and to show the importance of his part. He will ignore any dynamic markings. After all the composer may well have been deaf, so one shouldn't take his directions too literally.

Most second fiddles will have no idea what to do with a mute, and probably won't even own one. I remember lending a mute to a fellow player. It was not an insulting gesture on my part — the composer asked for it. After about five bars he tore it off, and hurled it across the room in a most aggressive manner. It narrowly missed a valuable porcelain vase, bearing the legend 'souvenir of Blackpool'.

At one time I played in a quartet with a particularly self-assertive second. Halfway through the session we were in the habit of breaking off for a light snack. One evening, when we resumed after the interval, we noticed immediately that he was playing with an uncharacteristic reserve. In fact he was practically inaudible. We wondered if he might be ill, because he had become very red in the face and was panting slightly. It quickly became obvious that he was extremely upset at being unable to produce his accustomed tone.

After about 30 seconds he stopped playing, and began wiping his bow with a handkerchief in a highly energetic way. He used quite a selection of unfamiliar words — no doubt obscure Italian musical terms.

Some butter had found its way onto the hair of his bow during the break, deadening the sound dramatically. He managed to remove some of it, but for the rest of the session his playing was unusually subdued.

For some reason none of us offered to lend him another bow. I can't imagine how we all failed to think of it.

By the next time we met he had got it clean again, and was playing as loudly as ever.

There are some good chamber works which require a piano, so turn on the charm for any keyboard players you meet.

Pianists are in the habit of playing alone, and it makes their counting suspect. They are also a serious liability when it comes to starting a

A View From The Stands

piece. They are quite likely to begin at a moment when the rest of you have your instruments on your knees. If this happens don't waste time trying to catch up with them. You won't manage it. Just pretend that you thought they were practising. After a few bars they invariably stop.

Personally I like to mix strings with wind now and then. Unfortunately there are not many good pieces, which no doubt accounts for the prejudice against wind I have encountered among string players. Most of the works that do exist are weighted strongly in favour of the wind — but they at least can manage the notes.

Chamber Music 2
Picking Up The Pieces

Having assembled a regular quartet, don't imagine that everything will then go smoothly.

If you organise chamber music evenings you will soon learn that from time to time players fail to turn up. You should therefore lay in a supply of music for small combinations. Cellists seem to be particularly unreliable. Perhaps the thought of lugging such heavy equipment about discourages them. Anyway, their absence will give you the biggest headaches.

One solution is to try and hold meetings at the cellist's home whenever possible. You could also try to overcome the problem by arranging quintets and sextets to allow for wastage. I think this is a mistake, because everyone will then turn up each time, and you quickly tire of the few available works. If eventually someone does drop out, it is certain both cellists or both violinists will let you down. There will then be nothing the rest of you can play.

Do not be fooled by people who leave virtuoso works, such as Paganini caprices, ostentatiously displayed on a music stand in the corner of the room. They are not learning them. In fact it's a pretty safe bet they haven't practised anything for months, and would be stretched if asked to play a C major scale.

It is a mistake to interfere with anyone's music, even if you are trying to be helpful.

A View From The Stands

There is a place in the Polka movement of Smetana's E Minor quartet where the viola has an impossible page turn mid-way through an important solo. At this stage the second violin is silent. During professional concerts I have seen the second fiddle lean over and turn his neighbour's page with an extrovert flourish.

On an evening when I found myself playing second in this work, I decided to adopt the same practice. I know the viola part pretty well — I hasten to add that this is quite a different matter from being able to play it — so I was able to time the turn perfectly.

Anne immediately stopped playing, and directed a contemptuous and disapproving glare in my direction.

'What on earth are you doing?' she demanded.

She is one of the most even-tempered people I know, but for once she seemed genuinely angry.

'I was just turning the page for you, so you wouldn't have to stop playing' I explained, and adopted one of those ingratiating smiles that have cost me friends from Surbiton to Scunthorpe.

'But I don't want the page turned' she protested.

I looked over her shoulder. The copy was unfamiliar. We were using an obscure edition, and sure enough the page turns were in quite different places.

I mumbled an apology, and we resumed.

Later in the evening, as she brought in the coffee, she managed to step on my foot. Somehow it evened the score, and relations returned to normal. She is a tall girl, and fortunately wears low heels.

One of my friends has a habit of throwing the windows open when we are playing. Unless you want to upset the people next door, you should keep the windows closed however hot the room becomes.

By and large passers-by do not take much notice of your efforts. The worst you should experience is a little derisory applause. With luck they may throw a few coins into the garden. Accept them gratefully, but don't rush out and collect them at once. It looks greedy. You are unlikely to make enough to influence your tax returns.

Very occasionally things can turn nasty. I recall an evening when children hurled stones at the window, but it was an isolated incident.

If strangers hang around outside for any length of time, don't be fooled into thinking that you have an appreciative audience. It's more likely they are representatives of the Noise Abatement Society gathering evidence.

A friend of mine, who has a higher opinion of his musical talent than those who have heard him play, noticed that people were starting to gather outside the window when he was playing a quartet in new surroundings. For a quarter of an hour his ego was boosted by this crowd of apparent admirers. Then a No. 11 bus pulled up and they all got on.

Amateur groups are usually very conservative in what they play. However I have encountered ambitious types.

I remember one girl who persuaded me to experiment with an extraordinary composition. The music was not written on a stave in the accepted way. Instead, each player had a single sheet of paper.

The top half was given over to a series of zig-zag lines. They could have been graphs showing a company's profits during a period of fluctuating fortunes. The bottom half consisted of a sequence of instructions on what to do.

Few people would have been able to induce me to attempt anything so bizarre, but Cheryl was one of those whose enthusiasm is infectious. She was a great champion of modern music, but even she agreed to abandon the attempt after a couple of minutes of aimless scratching and squeaking. It was a relief to go from that to Webern.

A couple of years later Cheryl suddenly married a military violinist — an unlikely combination — and vanished from our circle. She left a trail of broken hearts and moist handkerchiefs, and is sadly missed.

Her musical experiments are not.

If you feel the slightest urge to give a chamber music concert, there is

A View From The Stands

one important piece of advice that I would offer — and it comes absolutely free of charge. Don't!

Should you really believe you can carry it off, just try recording yourselves first. I guarantee you are in for a nasty shock.

If even this will not persuade you, at least include a pianist. For all their faults pianists do not play out of tune (though a good many pianos do), and so provide something tangible for the strings to relate to.

When playing with a piano, balance is particularly important. Professional groups like to have the piano lid almost closed, so that the other players can be heard. For amateurs the lid should be opened as wide as possible. The correct balance is for the piano to be so loud that everyone else is virtually inaudible. A good policy is to sabotage the instrument just before the performance, so that the loud pedal remains stuck on throughout.

Make no mistake — this is how the audience like it to be.

One of the most enjoyable things you can do is to go away to summer schools, or on weekend courses.

Usually you will be expected to come as a ready formed group, and that is by far the best policy. It is highly risky to go on your own, especially if there is a danger that you may be fixed up with the same people for the whole course. When players turn up alone it is frequently because those who know them can't face a whole week in their company. The reasons for this may differ, but will swiftly become apparent.

Before deciding who to go with, it is worth thinking about what you will do when you get there. Here, for instance, is my list of priorities:

1. Chatting up the opposite sex.
2. Testing the quality of the local brews.
3. Using any sporting facilities – indoors and out.
4. Getting away from the kids.
5. Having a lie in before breakfast.
6. Playing chamber music.
7. Finishing 'War and Peace'.

When forming your quartet it is essential to choose those who have similar interests. You don't have to agree on everything but the general outline should be the same.

I have known people who go away under the illusion that they are going to spend the whole time playing music. If you get involved with a set like that, you are in for a pretty lean time.

Even if you have no plans for a lie in, it is worth getting a room in as remote a part of the building as possible. There are always a few anti-social maniacs who insist on playing until one o'clock. A friend of mine went on a weekend course, and found she was sharing a bedroom not only with three other women, but also a piano. At about seven o'clock on Sunday morning the door was suddenly flung open, and a girl swept into the room and began practising Chopin. She was forcibly ejected. However the damage had been done, and in any case she found another instrument in the room directly below and hammered away until breakfast with her foot hard down on the loud pedal.

Resist the temptation to play in the open air. Apart from the unwelcome attentions of insects, it is a peculiarity of outdoor acoustics that, although you will disturb everyone within half a mile, you will be unable to hear each other. This means that there will be a total lack of ensemble.

String quartet courses are usually run by one-time professional quartets who have fallen on hard times. Make no mistake, if they could still get bookings to perform, they wouldn't be sitting around within earshot of amateurs. It is only because they need your money that they resist the temptation to speak truthfully at coaching sessions.

In order to get some measure of revenge, and because they are starved of real audiences, they will almost certainly choose to give a recital one evening. Their concert will be sure to end about 30 seconds after closing time.

If you dodge these performances it is unlikely to be noticed, and you certainly won't be missing anything worthwhile. But try not to burst into the room drunk while the concert is still in progress.

Finally, here is an example of the sort of evening you can look forward to if you invite some friends round to play quartets.

A View From The Stands

Mike, the cellist, is usually the first person to turn up. His prompt appearance might be mistaken for enthusiasm. It is an illusion. He is just getting out of the washing up. Playing quartets is a low priority occupation for him, an attitude well illustrated by his D string. It is repaired with a knot just inside the peg-box — a temporary measure that has lasted several months.

By about ten o'clock Mike will begin to pack up his cello ready to go. It's the agreed signal by which the evening is brought to a close. We will be given no other warning.

The leader, Norman, is the next to arrive. Although a tall man with enormous hands, he moves his fingers with a dexterity that would do credit to most professionals. Unfortunately a good deal of the advantage of this is lost, because his fingers rarely fall at exactly the right spot on the strings. He produces a thin and edgy tone. Between us we can easily drown his efforts. For most of the evening we will do so.

Harry, the second fiddle, is last to arrive. He is a heavily built man, and poses a serious threat to the furniture. He does not sit down in the accepted manner. He first hovers about the chair for a few seconds, and then removes the weight from his legs, allowing himself to land on it at considerable velocity.

Once we have settled into our places an attempt is made to tune up. Norman plays an A, using the point of his bow, and giving the string a series of gentle stabs. Harry takes long, deliberate strokes, and plays fortissimo.

They are about a semi-tone apart, and Norman tunes down to match his neighbour. While he is doing so, Harry is tuning up to join him. After this exercise they are exactly where they were to begin with, except that their positions have been reversed. The procedure is repeated a couple of times before a compromise is reached.

Meanwhile I have been practising a few octaves, choosing notes which clash with A, so that their task is made as difficult as possible.

There is now a short period of haggling over what we are going to play first. We invariably start with either Haydn or Mozart. Indeed, you will notice this with all amateur quartets, owing to the mistaken belief that these composers are relatively easy, and therefore good for warming up. If warming up is supposed to result in any noticeable improvement, the exercise is in vain.

This evening it is to be Mozart, and we select the quartet in G Major.

The first breakdown of the session occurs early in the first movement. It is brought about by Harry's shoulder rest, which collapses and falls noisily to the floor.

Although a successful and efficient business man, he has never proved himself sufficiently well organised to either repair or replace it. For most of the ten years we have been playing together it has provided occasional interruptions.

There is a second stoppage when we reach the first double bar. Apart from the fact that we do not all arrive at this mile-stone together, we have not come to a decision about repeating the opening section. We never decide such matters in advance, so this is a predictable halt. After a short discussion it is Norman who wins the day. He is an optimist, and favours repeating. It is his opinion that it can only be better a second time — a prediction that we emphatically disprove.

During the development section we run into some problems with the ensemble. It requires several more restarts before we eventually stagger to the end of the movement.

The Minuet is reasonably straightforward, and for once no-one gets lost. However we become aware of some curious and disturbing harmonies throughout the Trio. Towards the end I suddenly realise that I am to blame. I have disregarded the modulation to G Minor. To compensate for my lapse I stay in the Minor when we repeat the Minuet. At least it keeps the whole movement in character.

The Andante presents the leader with some technical challenges. In his anxiety to get past the blacker passages he accelerates, thus making things worse. Fortunately the other three parts are relatively simple, and we manage to keep with him.

The quartet ends with a Fugue. This might be expected to cause us some additional difficulties. However we have our own method of dealing with it. By taking it at about half the speed Mozart had in mind, we reach the end easily. Much pleased with ourselves, we break for a drink.

After a couple of pints we have enough courage to read through a Dvorak quartet in E Flat. Dvorak is more in our style. We can get away with plenty of Rubato. For us, of course, Rubato means slowing down whenever things get a bit tricky. As we don't all have technical problems at the same time there are frequent discrepancies between the parts. They tend to average out, so that every couple of minutes we play a bar together.

A curious incident occurs in the last movement. After a slow passage there is a final 'A Tempo'. This goes disasterously wrong. Instead of starting there we decide to get a feel for the tempo change by beginning two bars earlier. We then all sit and look around expectantly from face to face, waiting for something to happen. Eventually we realise that we all have two bars rest, so in the end we begin at the 'A Tempo' after all. And so another quartet comes to a shaky end.

Before breaking up we decide that next time we will work on a Beethoven quartet, and the parts are handed out so we can look at them. You may be sure when we meet no-one will have opened his part, and we will probably have forgotten what we planned to do. Even if we remember, at least one of us will have come without the music, so there is no danger of it being played.

Tailpiece
Some Sharp Practice

You may have noticed that I have said nothing about practising. There is a good reason for this. Amateurs as a rule do not practise — at least not the notes.

However, if you join an orchestra it is worth spending a little time preparing some of the techniques outlined earlier. For instance, you could devote some time to turning pages. After a few goes, you should be able to spin a turn out to as much as ten seconds.

Having mastered the technical side, it's worth paying some attention to facial expressions. You will need a mirror for this. You could try the effect of raising and lowering one eyebrow, developing an interesting twitch, etc. But resist the temptation to save time by shaving while you are doing this. Not only are some of the best effects hidden by foam, but you could end up with a nasty gash.

Sometimes you might go to a concert given by musicians. Just occasionally they resort to the ploys used by Bluffers, and it is gratifying to be able to spot them. I might have more to say on that, but it will require another book.

Coda

Here is a list of chamber works for strings that you should avoid. It should not be adhered to too rigidly. A degree of prejudice may have crept in.

Bartok String Quartets 1 to 6 — Even if you were to play them correctly, which you won't, they sound like cats fighting in a hail storm.

A View From The Stands

Beethoven String Quartet Opus 132 — Anyone who can stay awake through the interminable slow movement must suffer from insomnia. (The other movements are not too bad.)

String Quartet Opus 133 (Die Grosse Fuge) — This may be a good exercise for playing dotted rhythms, but musically it is a monstrosity. It's practically unplayable anyway. (Die Grosse Fuge is not German for 'The Great Bore', although you might be forgiven for thinking so. The Great Boar is a popular constellation, and has nothing to do with music.)

Berg Lyric Suite (for string quartet) — No need to buy the music of this piece, since the notes are completely random.

Boccherini String Quintets (the lot) — Some early examples of computer aided design.

Borodin String Quartet No. 2 — The second quartet is based on some third rate musical. Or maybe some musical is based on this third rate quartet. It all comes to the same thing anyway.

Brahms String Quartet No. 3 — The first movement is devoid of musical ideas. Instead it is full of unplayable cross-rhythms. The third movement is marvellous — if you happen to be a violist.

Bruckner String Quintet — It takes nearly an hour, and contains only one good idea. When this does finally arrive it is set in E Flat Minor, so you won't be able to play it.

Debussy String Quartet — A typical piece of French music. It goes nowhere, and stretches your technique on the way. The French should stick to what they understand — cuisine.

Dvorak String Quartet Opus 105 — Anyone who opens a quartet in A Flat Minor cannot seriously expect to have it played.

Haydn String Quartet Opus 76 No. 6 — The final two movements are just a series of scales (a description I would have liked to have been able to apply to the Trout Quintet). It is one of the most blatant examples of note spinning I have come across.

Mendelssohn   String Octet — This would be a good piece if seven of the participants were to play pianissimo at any one time. They never do.

Mozart   String Quintet in C Major — This is a great romp for the first fiddle and first viola. It is no joke for the other three.

Puccini   Chrysanthemum Quartet — Sentimentality run riot. Almost as big a yawn as Madame Butterfly. Puccini is reported to have composed it in a single night. That's just the way it sounds.

Ravel   String Quartet — See Debussy.

Schubert   String Quartet in D Minor (Death and the Maiden) — Only suitable for athletes in peak condition. Do not attempt the Finale if you have a heart condition. You'd be wise to keep a bucket of water handy, in case your bow bursts into flames.

Schumann   Piano Quintet — Another work based on a musical. You will need a third hand to deal with the scherzo — obtainable at all good hardware shops.

Shostakovich   Piano Quintet — This is not really a quintet, but a piece for five unrelated instruments. It illustrates the composer's conviction that pianists have only one finger.

Smetana   String Quartet No. 2 — A nasty attack of E Major, though not officially until the Finale. Not that anyone could really be expected to play those arpeggios in any key.

Tchaikovsky   String Sextet — Although nominally scored for six players, it is really written for full orchestra.